Guess Who?

By Anne W. Ball

Illustrations by Lois Axeman

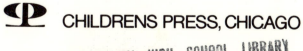

CHILDRENS PRESS, CHICAGO

About the author:
Anne W. Ball lives in Columbus, Georgia, with her husband, a US Army helicopter pilot. As a teacher sensitive to the needs of students in the social studies field, Mrs. Ball started writing for her own classroom. Mr. and Mrs. Ball have one child and enjoy travel and art collecting.

About the Artist:
Lois Axeman is a native Chicagoan who lives with her husband and two children in the city. After attending the American Academy and the Institute of Design (IIT), Lois started as a fashion illustrator in a department store. When the childrens wear illustrator became ill, Lois took her place and found she loved drawing children. She started free-lancing then, and has been doing text and picture books ever since.

Library of Congress Catalog Card Number: 70-178487

1 2 3 4 5 6 7 8 9 10 11 12 13 14 15 16 17 18 19 20 21 22 23 24 25 R 75 74 73 72

At break of day he grabs his coat,
And takes his crew out in the boat.
Dragging nets of heavy twine,
He catches food that's really fine.
He works hard as you can see,
And makes his living from the sea.

GUESS WHO?

FISHERMAN

She's the girl who helps the boss.
Without her he is at a loss.
A pretty smile for all to see,
She works hard for her company.
Typing, filing or on the phone,
It's through these duties she is known.

GUESS WHO?

SECRETARY

He spends long hours in the field,
Working so his plants will yield.
His rake and hoe help him to sow.
The healthful foods that we all know.
Melons large or onions small,
He's the man who grows them all.

GUESS WHO?

FARMER

In the courtroom of the town,
This man wears a long black gown.
He works with lawyers and police.
To guard the law and keep the peace.
Very honest, smart and just,
He quickly earns respect and trust.

GUESS WHO?

JUDGE

He drives for miles on the road,
Hauling a most important load.
He's the man who daily brings,
Food and clothes and other things.
Because of him there will be more
Goods to buy at your nearby store.

GUESS WHO?

TRUCK DRIVER

Day after day she stands in line,
Helping to make the goods so fine.
She tightens only one small screw,
But she's important to the crew.
You can buy the things she makes:
A clock, a car or roller skates!

GUESS WHO?

FACTORY WORKER

A pole with stripes is near his door,
To show the way into his store.
If you have some hair to spare,
Come and sit in his big chair.
With comb and shears he earns his pay.
He cuts your hair your favorite way.

GUESS WHO?

BARBER

With his badge and coat of blue,
He is my friend and your friend, too.
His courage guards both you and me,
And keeps our city safe and free.
Brave and friendly, he's the man
Who's paid to give a helping hand.

GUESS WHO?

POLICEMAN

Saw and hammer in his hand,
He builds things just as they were
   planned.
He uses tools as he must,
And always cleans the floor of dust.
A door, a window, floor or chair,
He takes his time and works with care.

GUESS WHO?

CARPENTER

He's the man you go to see
When you are sick as sick can be.
He often thinks a shot or pill
Is quite the thing to cure your ill.
Even though *you* doubt it might,
His medicine you'll find is right.

GUESS WHO?

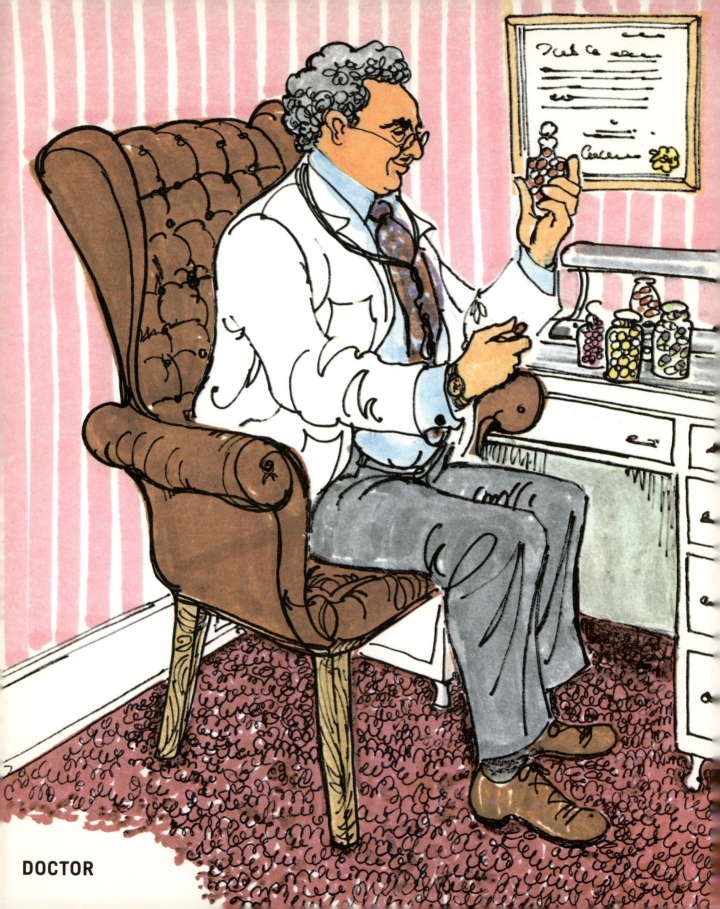

DOCTOR

He wears white from shoes to hat,
Mixing dough in a great big vat.
Working long into the night,
He bakes our bread so good and light.
He takes his time so he will learn
Not to let your pastries burn!

GUESS WHO?

BAKER

When a fire comes your way,
This brave man will earn his pay.
Quick to face the flame and fire,
His strength and spirit we admire.
When fires start by day or night,
He battles them with all his might.

GUESS WHO?

He is a fireman. What does he do?

When all the workers go away,
This friendly man will start his day.
Armed with bucket, mop and broom,
He cleans the dust from every room.
In the morning his work is done.
Wasn't he a busy one?

GUESS WHO?

JANITOR

In her classroom every day,
She makes learning seem like play.
When asked a question, you will see,
She always seems to know the key.
Teaching you what you should know
Will always help you as you grow.

GUESS WHO?

CHART

TEACHER

Through the clouds high in the sky
You see his silver plane glide by.
He travels fast from town to town,
But then lands safely on the ground.
Wearing a cap and suit of blue,
He leads the members of his crew.

GUESS WHO?

PILOT